Ancient Greek Children

Richard Tames

Heinemann LIBRARY

www.heinemann.co.uk/library
Visit our website to find out more information about **Heinemann Library** books.

To order:
☎ Phone 44 (0) 1865 888066
▤ Send a fax to 44 (0) 1865 314091
▣ Visit the Heinemann Bookshop at www.heinemann.co.uk/library to browse our catalogue and order online.

First published in Great Britain by Heinemann Library, Halley Court, Jordan Hill, Oxford OX2 8EJ, a division of Reed Educational and Professional Publishing Ltd. Heinemann is a registered trademark of Reed Educational & Professional Publishing Limited.

OXFORD MELBOURNE AUCKLAND JOHANNESBURG BLANTYRE
GABORONE IBADAN PORTSMOUTH NH (USA) CHICAGO

Designed by Tinstar Design (www.tinstar.co.uk)
Illustration by Art Construction.
Originated by Ambassador Litho Ltd.
Printed by Wing King Tong in Hong Kong.

ISBN 0 431 14550 4 (hardback)   ISBN 0 431 14553 9 (paperback)
06 05 04 03 02   07 06 05 04 03
10 9 8 7 6 5 4 3 2 1   10 9 8 7 6 5 4 3 2 1

British Library Cataloguing in Publication Data
Tames, Richard
    Ancient Greek children. – (People in the past)
    1. Children – Greece – History – To 1500 – Juvenile literature
    2. Civilization – Modern – Greek influences – Juvenile literature
    3. Greece – Civilization – To 146 B.C. – Juvenile literature
    I.Title
    938

Acknowledgements
The Publishers would like to thank the following for permission to reproduce photographs:
AKG London pp8, 12, 21, 22, 24, 26, 30, 32, 36, 40, 41, Ancient Art and Architecture Collection pp6, 7, 10, 14, 16, 18, 31, 33, 34, Bildarchive Preussicher Kulturbesitz p25, British Museum p38, Michael Holford p28, Richard Butler and Magnet Harlequin p43, Werner Forman Archive pp11, 42.

Cover photograph reproduced with permission of Ancient Art and Architecture Collection.

Every effort has been made to contact copyright holders of any material reproduced in this book. Any omissions will be rectified in subsequent printings if notice is given to the Publishers.

The Publishers would like to thank Dr Michael Vickers of the Ashmolean Museum, Oxford, for his assistance in the preparation of this book.

Words appearing in the text in bold, **like this**, are explained in the glossary.

Contents

The world of the ancient Greeks

When people talk about ancient Greece, they do not just mean the modern-day country of Greece as it used to be. The ancient-Greek world was made up of the hot, rocky mainland of Greece, plus hundreds of islands in the Aegean, Ionian and Adriatic Seas, with further overseas settlements in places ranging from northern Africa to what we now call Turkey and Italy. The earliest Greek-speakers did not think they all belonged to a single country. For a long while they did not even think they all belonged to the same **civilization**.

For centuries the mightiest people in the Greek world were the Minoans, based on the island of Crete. Power then passed to the warlike Mycenaeans, based on the mainland region known as the **Peloponnese**. This was followed around the year 1100 BC by centuries of confusion and upheaval. In the later 'Classical Age', from about 500 BC until about 300 BC, prosperity was restored by the rise of many city-states like Athens and Sparta. The Greek word for city-state was **_polis_**. Each _polis_ controlled the villages and farmland around it.

What we owe to the Greeks

We look back to ancient Greece as the origin of the Western civilization that has evolved in Europe, North America and elsewhere. Greeks invented **democracy**, drama and trial by jury. The Greeks were curious and willing to learn from the **Babylonians**, the Egyptians and the peoples of neighbouring Asia Minor (modern Turkey). After Greece became part of the Roman Empire, the Romans valued the Greek language and Greek learning and passed them on to future generations.

Forming our language

Thousands of Greek words have passed into other European languages. Angel and asthma, arthritis and automatic are all Greek words. So are chorus and cycle, **martyr** and museum, police and politics. Modern words like 'technology' are still made up from Greek: _techne_ (craft or know how) + _logos_ (word or science).

500 874369

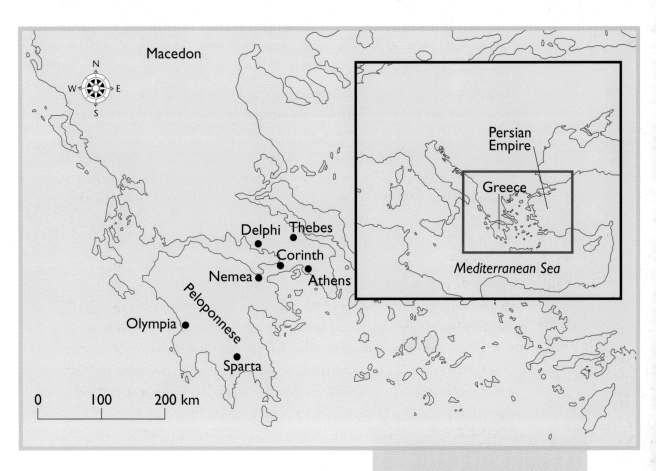

This book is about children in ancient Greece, so it is about becoming a Greek and everything that meant – learning the language, customs and beliefs handed on from one generation to the next. Nowadays it is often said that 'our children are the future'. The ancient Greeks had tremendous confidence in the Greek way of life, but in their world they cannot have been so confident about the survival of their own family. Greeks often died young, either from untreatable diseases or in wars between the city-states. This meant that attitudes to childhood were often very different from those we know today.

Ancient Greece was not a single unified country but a collection of many separate states that often waged war on one another. The ancient Greeks used the word *Hellas* to mean all the places where there was a Greek way of life.

Invisible children

The problem of the past

Historians try to build a picture of the past out of the things people made and the documents they wrote. These two sorts of evidence help each other out. Most of the evidence we have, however, was made or written down by adults. So it can often be difficult to find out about the lives of children who lived more than 2000 years ago.

The Parthenon is a **temple** in Athens **dedicated** to the city's **guardian**, the goddess Athene. Athene was just one of the many gods and goddesses worshipped by the ancient Greeks. There is a carved **frieze** around the Parthenon showing girls presenting a new dress to the goddess. From written sources we also know young girls wove the dress as well. This helps us to understand how the Greeks thought about girlhood. Young girls were thought to be pure and innocent, possibly because Greek society was run by men, meaning that boys had to worry about less pure things like war and money. Because of this, girls were also thought best fitted to **weave** a dress for a goddess and to present it to her in person on behalf of the whole community.

Making things

Examples like the Parthenon frieze are rather unusual. Children growing up in ancient Greece often helped adults to build houses or make pottery as they learned these trades from their elders. The resulting products, however, were still essentially designed and made by adults. The child's contribution – fetching tools or helping to mix clay – remains invisible.

This vase gives information about adult life, but a child may have been involved in making it.

We cannot, therefore, learn much about the children of ancient Greece from what they made or helped to make. We can learn something from what was made for them, such as toys, and from what was made about them, such as paintings or carvings showing children.

Words

Only a minority of Greek children learned to read and write. Examples of how and what they were supposed to learn have survived. Yet children did not write about themselves. When they were old enough to do so, they were no longer children.

Thinking about childhood

Some important Greek thinkers, like Plato and Aristotle, did write about children, but they wrote mainly about how children ought to be brought up, not about how they actually were. Plato and Aristotle may well have been childless, with no direct experience from children of their own. Plato did, however, realize that how children learned to play could have a powerful effect on forming their character as adults.

Women were closest to children because they spent much more time with them than men did. Greek homes were divided into areas for men and areas for women. Until they were about six years old both boys and girls spent nearly all their time in the women's quarters of a Greek home.

A huge Greek theatre – but drama was meant for adults.

Being born

Danger and delight

Childbirth in ancient Greece was very risky. Wives were expected to have one baby after another. A wife unable to bear children thought herself cursed by the gods and was pitied by other women. A girl who died before having children was thought to have lived to no purpose. Repeated childbirth often weakened mothers and increased the danger of later births. About half of all women died by the age of 40. Because husbands were usually much older than wives, few men lived to see their grandchildren grow up. Childbirth involved blood, and the Greeks believed that the spilling of blood in the home left the household **ritually polluted**. Anyone visiting it would be unable to visit a **temple** for three days afterwards.

This statue from around 375 BC shows an old nurse with a baby. It would probably only have been wealthy families that had nurses or 'nannies' looking after their children.

The father, naked, carried a new baby on a circuit around the house. Friends and family sent gifts. The doorway of the home was decorated with a **wreath** of olives, for a boy, or a wreath of wool for a girl. Greek families wanted boys not girls. A boy would **inherit** family property, carry on the family name and become a warrior for his *polis*. A girl had to be married off and that usually meant paying a **dowry**.

To live or to die

A new baby was anxiously examined for 'defects'. A loud cry was taken as a very healthy sign. Sickly or deformed children, especially girls, were often left out to die. A crooked limb or even red hair might be thought to show the gods were angry for some reason. The child might be a burden on the family and give birth to other 'damaged' children. Children who were not 100 per cent fit were not always thrown away, however, especially a first-born male.

Names

Greek children were given only one name. This might refer to a god or goddess (Herodotus – meaning given by Hera), an animal (Philippos or Philip – meaning lover of horses), a plant (Phyllis – meaning a green bough). Some names reflected family pride – Cleopatra means 'glory of her father' and Demosthenes means 'the people's strength'. In public a person might be called by their father's name as well – 'son of ...' and also by the village they came from. The first male child was often named after his father's father, the second after his mother's father, the third after one of his father's uncles and so on. Any nickname a person got as an adult remained personal and was not handed on to children.

Bringing up baby

The ancient Greeks did not think of babies as cute little angels who should be marvelled at, fussed over and spoiled with gifts and treats. A baby was everything that an adult man should not be. It was physically weak, stupid, easily fooled and without either memory or self-control. All these qualities had to be instilled into the baby by its upbringing to make it into a satisfactory adult. A satisfactory adult was a man who could fight to defend his city and take part in running it. All that was required of girls was that they grow up obedient and able to run a house and bear children.

Myths of childhood

Some favourite Greek **myths** told stories about extraordinary babies whose amazing deeds showed that they would one day become heroes. When Hercules was born, the jealous goddess Hera was said to have sent snakes to kill him in his cradle – but baby Hercules simply strangled them! This story fitted in with the story that Hercules had enormous strength – even as a baby. The warrior Achilles was said to have killed a wild boar when he was only six. Alexander the Great, who became a real hero, was supposed to have tamed his famous horse, Bucephalus, while he was only a boy.

This kind of clay pot kept a baby from harm or mischief in the house and served as a potty at the same time.

The popularity of these stories shows how much the Greeks admired tough fighters, whether they were gods or humans. The Athenian politician Hyperides said 'We educate children so that they may become good men and they show that they were well educated as children by being especially brave in battle.'

Method

The **philosopher** Plato had very definite views on child-rearing. Like many Greeks he thought that because babies had soft skin and flexible bones, they should be wrapped up tightly until they were two years old to make sure their joints grew strong and their limbs straight. For the same reason they should be carried around until they were three, rather than being made to walk too early – nowadays, toddlers are encouraged to walk as soon as possible.

When Greek children did walk, though, they should go barefoot to toughen their feet. From three years old until six they should be put to play with other children. By the age of seven, when their baby teeth had fallen out and been replaced, they should be ready to begin their education and boys should be separated from girls.

Greek children usually grew up in large households where aunts, female slaves and older sisters as well as their own mothers helped bring them up. This carving might be showing any one of these different carers.

Home comforts

Keep it simple

Most Greek homes were one-storey houses made of sun-dried mud brick, with thick walls, small, shuttered windows and an open, airy **courtyard**, off which there were rooms such as bedrooms, storerooms and the kitchen. The grandest room was a dining room used for male guests or family **ceremonies**. Children would normally be kept out of this room. Even wealthy homes had only wooden-framed beds, couches, stools and chests for storage. Country houses were often larger because land was cheaper in the country.

Courtyard life

The courtyard was the focus of family life and where girls and women passed most of their time. It let light and air into rooms that would otherwise be cool and dingy. Cooking on portable **hearths** or **braziers** could be done outside in warm weather, which was much more pleasant than in a hot, smoke-filled kitchen. Small children could play safely in the courtyard with their friends or animals. There was also room for doing messy jobs, like washing sheep's fleeces.

Here, a boy calls to his dog. Dogs would have been used to guard homes at night and to protect sheep from wolves.

Greek houses were divided into different areas for men and women. Children were usually looked after by their mothers so, naturally, they would spend most of their time in the female part of the house, as well as the courtyard. Men often entertained guests in their part of the house and it would have been a big step in a young man's life when he was invited to these parties. Girls would move to the house of their husband when they married.

Daily bread

The Greeks divided food into two sorts. *Sitos* was bread, biscuit, cake or porridge, made from wheat or barley, often with beans, peas, lentils or lupins mixed in. *Sitos* was meant to fill you up. *Opson* was whatever relish was put on it, such as olive oil or salt. Fish and shellfish, rather than meat, provided **protein** in the Greek diet. Meat was only eaten after being **sacrificed** to the gods. It was a special treat for special days. Children rarely ate it.

Fresh bread or porridge was made daily, so grinding wheat or barley into flour was a regular chore for girls. Milk was used for cheese, rather than as a drink. Girls regularly helped their mothers with baking, milking, cheesemaking and pressing olives for their oil. They also gathered nuts, berries and honey, which was the only sweetener.

Did the Greeks keep pets?

Greek children came into contact with animals, particularly if they lived in the country, but they would probably not have understood modern attitudes towards pets. Although there are pictures that show children playing with dogs, these animals would have had a practical use. In the countryside, men used dogs to hunt for food.

Clothes and fashions

The weather in Greece is normally warm and dry, although some of the more mountainous areas can be cold in winter. The clothes that ancient-Greek children wore did not need to be too warm because the weather was so hot.

Materials

Both cloth and clothes were made at home by the mother of the family, helped by her daughters and slaves. This was true of the rich as well as of ordinary families. The main materials were wool and linen. Girls first learned to spin wool into yarn. Then they learned to **weave** yarn into cloth on a loom, to make garments, blankets, cushions and wall-hangings.

This carving shows the long, flowing lines of typical garments.

Making linen was a long business but each stage was simple enough for children to help out with. **Flax** plants were gathered by hand, tied in bundles, dried out, combed to take out the seed capsules and soaked in water to separate out the fibres. The fibres were beaten to soften them, then washed and spun into yarn to be woven. In fine linen, the flax fibres were thinner and less rough. Coarse linen was used for bags or aprons, fine linen for things like underwear or **tunics**, which needed to be smoother because they were worn next to the skin. Most materials were undyed. Richer people wore clothes coloured with dyes made from plants.

Finding out about clothes

Although no clothes have survived from the time, most of what we know about Greek children's clothing comes from writings and paintings on vases. Often, though, Greeks were shown naked on vases, to distinguish them from foreigners who are shown wearing clothes. This makes it even more difficult to find out what Greek children wore. Statues tell us a lot about clothing and hairstyles but they cannot usually tell us about the colours of clothes – if they were painted, in most cases the paint has worn off long ago.

Garments

There was little difference between the clothes worn by males and females of whatever age. Styles changed little over centuries. Mothers and daughters both wore an ankle-length loose dress, girdled at the waist and pinned at the shoulder. Girls wore white until they were married. Boys wore a knee-length tunic, men a longer one. In cold weather, cloaks or shawls were worn. In Sparta, where the army was all-important, boys wore only a thin cloak and went barefoot all year round to toughen them up.

The most usual footwear in Greece was leather sandals. Children and countryfolk often went barefoot. Both girls and boys let their hair grow long but often braided it to keep it out of the way.

Family life

Father knows best

The Greeks had no word for family in the common modern sense. Instead they referred to the group of related people who lived together as an **oikos** – a household. A Greek household included not only a married couple and their children but also their slaves, animals, land, house, buildings and sometimes other relatives, such as aged grandparents and unmarried female relatives. In big cities, it might also include lodgers or temporary residents. All came under the authority of the male head of the household.

In this farewell scene, a mother (seated) says goodbye to her daughter. Girls would leave the family home to be married.

One, big, happy family
Greeks liked large families. Family members could help each other in work and politics, so the bigger a family the richer and more powerful it could become. The more children one had, the better chance there was that some would survive to look after their parents when they were old. If a married couple failed to have children of their own, or lost them through illness or accident, they often adopted others so that there was someone to **inherit** their property, carry on the family name and look after their tomb when they died. Fathers who only had daughters might adopt a son-in-law for these reasons, as in ancient-Greek times, a daughter would not inherit the family property.

Mother dearest
The duty of the mother was to have children, bring them up and organize the household. Girls married in their early teens, often to men who might be twenty years older. As a result of repeated childbirth and possibly because they were sometimes not as well fed as men, many wives died in their twenties or thirties. As a result, husbands might have remarried two or three times. This meant many children were brought up by stepmothers and, among the rich, by nurses or nannies. When a woman was left a widow she usually went to live with a male relative. If she was still young she would be encouraged to remarry.

Sparta was different!

A soldier society

Sparta was different from every other Greek city-state because it was organized for war as a way of life. All ordinary work in Sparta was done by slaves called *helots*. Spartan men were the only full-time army in ancient Greece. Spartan boys grew up knowing they had only one future – as a soldier.

Fit to live?

Every boy child was inspected at birth to see if he was fit to live. A panel of older men, not the baby's father, made the decision. Sickly or deformed babies were left in a mountain gorge to die of starvation or cold. Spartan mothers washed their babies in wine, not water, because they believed this would strengthen them.

Training for war

At seven years of age boys left their family to live in **barracks**. They learned a little reading and writing but most time was spent on gymnastics, athletics and rough team games led by older boys. They also learned marching songs and a special kind of dancing as a preparation for **military drill**. From twelve onwards it got even harder.

This Spartan soldier from the 6th century BC wears a crested helmet to make him look taller. Boys would have to get used to wearing such a helmet, which protected the cheeks and nose. Also, soldiers wore close-fitting armour to protect their chests and lower legs.

Boys were deliberately kept short of food to learn how to endure hunger and practise stealing it – a useful skill in wartime – but being caught stealing led to a savage beating. Weapons training focused on handling the **infantry's** 3 metre spear and heavy bronze shield. Spartans thought the **cavalry** was for weaklings and **archery** was for cowards.

Grown up

Spartan youths spent their last teenage year training younger boys. At twenty they were allowed to grow long hair and were elected to a **mess** of about fifteen men. They would eat and live with this group. From 30 onwards they were allowed to have a say in politics. By 30 they should have married and begun to have children but would remain with their mess, not their wife, until they were over 60.

Tough girls

Spartan girls had to learn to be tough, just like the boys. We know that Spartan girls trained as athletes. In other city-states, athletics was mostly for the men. Girls had to learn to control their household. Because Spartan men spent so much time training and fighting, girls and women had to learn to manage on their own.

Treatment of toddlers

Plutarch, a Roman writing in the 2nd century AD, described how infants were brought up in Sparta:

'... They were not closely wrapped up but grew freely ... ate whatever they were given; were not afraid of the dark or being left alone; and not allowed tantrums or sulking or crying. For this reason Spartan nurses were often ... hired by people of other countries ...'

The world of work

Perhaps because so much hard and heavy work was done by slaves, the Greeks did not respect it. Instead they admired men with leisure time for education, poetry, sport and politics. Wealthy Greeks thought craftsmen were little better than the slaves they worked with – although they did admire their wonderful skills.

Helping at home

Children, especially in poor families without slaves, were expected to help out at home. Regular jobs included looking after younger children, gathering **fodder** and fuel, clearing stones from fields and throwing them at birds to protect the crops. Because Greece has little good **grazing land**, it was more common to keep goats and sheep than cows. As they are much smaller than cows it was easier to put boys in charge of herding them. In the autumn, boys would climb the olive trees to shake the ripe olives to the ground.

Water was needed for washing and cooking as well as drinking, so fetching it from a river, well or fountain might have been done several times a day. Because respectable females were supposed to stay inside their home, boys were usually sent on errands or used as messengers. Girls might look after the hens that stayed close to the house. Most girls learned from their mother how to cook, clean, **weave** cloth, nurse family members when they were sick and generally keep a home. Even girls in wealthy families were expected to do this to show they were respectable and could supervise slaves – making sure that they were doing household tasks properly.

Defending the city

When fathers went away to war, older boys were expected to take charge of the slaves left behind and make sure they still did their work properly. In a city under attack, boys were expected to support its defenders by passing **ammunition** to the fighting front – such as arrows and stones for slings and **catapults** – and to help re-build damaged walls.

Do it like dad

Many boys did not go to school but were brought up to do whatever jobs their father did, learning the trade from him. Farmer's sons became farmers; craftsmen's sons became craftsmen. Most businesses were small workshops, where a man worked with his sons and one or two slaves, almost never more than ten people in all. The largest business ever recorded in ancient Greece had 120 employees, making shields, but these were all slaves.

Girls would stay at home and learn how to run a home. Some may also have learned the art of Greek dancing, illustrated here by these statues.

Slavery

Slavery was common throughout the Greek world, particularly in Athens. A free Athenian without even one slave was thought of as poor.

Where did slaves come from?

Slavery was an alternative to killing captured prisoners of war. Often the men of a conquered city would be killed and the women and children sold off to traders, who followed armies around just to buy prisoners. Prisoners were sold to pay for the huge costs of war, which the **citizens** often had to pay themselves. Other slaves were bought from pirates who had kidnapped them. Children and teenagers were most in demand because they were easier to control and train and had a lifetime's work in them. Sometimes adults were temporarily enslaved until they could pay off a debt. If they could not pay, their children could become slaves, too. Some slaves were babies that had been abandoned at birth. Anyone rescuing such a baby could bring it up as a slave. Most slaves were simply born as children of slaves.

This painting shows a slave using a yoke to carry large jars. Jars like these might have been used to store wine or olive oil.

How were slaves treated?

A small number of slaves were owned by governments and worked as policemen, clerks, porters and messengers. Most, especially child slaves, worked in households, helping with daily chores like cleaning, washing and cooking. Very bright slave children might be taught to read and write. Although household slaves could be beaten it was not in their owner's interest to treat them harshly. Unhappy and unhealthy slaves worked badly. They could also damage things and even poison their owners! In very rich families slaves were often given positions of trust as **physician**, teacher, bookkeeper or bodyguard. Some Greeks disapproved of letting slaves get too involved in bringing up their children. Because most slaves were not Greek, the child might learn foreign ideas and pick up bad manners or ways of speaking.

The lives of slave children depended greatly on their parents' good behaviour. An owner could always sell a slave's children out of the household as a punishment. Just knowing he could do this was usually enough to keep their obedience.

Freedom

Some slaves were allowed to run their own businesses and use the money they made to buy their freedom. These 'freedmen' in Athens had the same limited rights as foreign residents but their children could enjoy full citizen rights, such as owning property and voting in elections.

Hard labour

Slaves were also used to mass-produce weapons and household goods such as pottery, beds and knives. Over 30,000 slaves worked the silver mines at Laurion, owned by the Athenian government. Many of them were children, because they were small enough to crawl into and work in narrow tunnels. They were treated very badly because they were not part of a household and it was not in their masters' interests to treat them well. There were many accidents, which could cause serious injury or death.

Education

Private fee-paying schools existed in Greece by about 500 BC. No law required that children go to school. There were schools for girls but not many. The Greeks believed that girls could learn all they needed to know about running a household in the family home – there was no need for them to go to school.

In Athens, boys from poorer homes went to school aged seven for about three or four years to master basic **literacy**. Boys from better-off homes might go for up to ten years, starting at an earlier age and finishing later. The richer ones went with a trusted slave who made sure they stuck to their studies and reported back to their parents each day. Classes were usually small, up to twelve. Pupils who did badly were beaten with a stick.

What was taught at school?

There were three kinds of teacher. One taught reading, writing, arithmetic and literature, which meant learning long passages of poetry, particularly by the poet Homer (see page 27), by heart. Stories of the great heroes of the past were supposed to make boys want to grow up to be brave too.

Here a music teacher listens to his pupil play the pipes. The music master's lyre can be seen behind the boy's head.

This painted cup from around 500 BC shows a school scene from ancient Greece. We can see a lesson in playing the lyre (left) and reading aloud from a scroll (right).

The second was a sports coach, who supervised wrestling, gymnastics and athletics. The third was a music master who taught the **lyre**, singing and chanting rhythmic poetry. Children from poorer homes may have missed out on this sort of education. The very rich might have a tutor at home but would probably still go to the local gymnasium for sports coaching and to the music master as well. This would enable them to take part in competitions – a constant feature of school and public life. Greeks liked winners!

Writing instruments and materials

The earliest Greek writings were scratched onto clay tablets or written on animal skins that had been scraped and stitched together as a continuous roll. By 600 BC the Greeks had begun to buy papyrus from Egypt. This was a kind of paper made from strips of pith from the reeds that grew along the river Nile. As these reeds would not grow in Greece, the Greeks were forced to go on importing the papyrus. Reed pens were used to write on it, with ink made from soot and vegetable gum. From 200 BC onwards the Greeks also began to use parchment, made from animal skins scraped as smooth as papyrus. As these materials were expensive, learners began to practise their letters in sand trays and then moved on to scratching them with a bronze or bone stylus on wax tablets, which could be melted smooth and used again.

Reading, writing and reciting

Literacy

In rich city-states like Athens most male **citizens** could probably read and write. There are no **statistics** to prove this, but plenty of evidence to suggest it. Each year Athenians could vote to send an unpopular citizen into **exile** for ten years. This was called 'ostracism' because the names of candidates were scratched on a bit of broken pottery called an *ostrakon*. Any voter had to be able to write a name at least. Large numbers of **inscriptions** and graffiti have been found scratched on walls. These were often like modern advertisements or road signs and they were designed to be read by as many people as possible. This suggests that many people could read a bit. Even so, most foreign residents, women and slaves were probably **illiterate**.

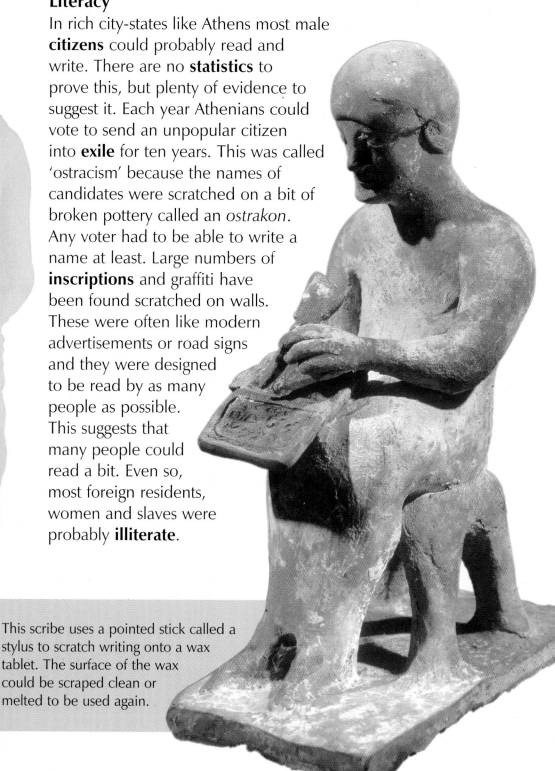

This scribe uses a pointed stick called a stylus to scratch writing onto a wax tablet. The surface of the wax could be scraped clean or melted to be used again.

Tall tales

Soon after the Greeks adopted an alphabet, in around 800 BC, two ancient epic poems, the *Iliad* and the *Odyssey*, were written down. These great adventure stories thrilled Greek children with tales of sea monsters and one-eyed giants. The Greeks thought they were made up by a blind poet called Homer long ago. Some modern scholars think Homer was actually several people whose separate stories were mixed together. The poems were meant to be told aloud, rather than read, so people could enjoy them together. Although these poems had been written down, copies would have to be written out by hand and would have been extremely expensive – Greek children would have learnt most things by heart from the teacher rather than from books.

Speak up!

Greeks loved talking and admired people who could recite or make speeches well. Schoolboys learned poems and famous speeches by heart. The cleverest ones then studied the art of public speaking, which Greeks called 'rhetoric'. Rich young Athenians who wanted to go into politics paid a tutor called a *sophist* to improve their skill in arguing. They learned to control nervousness, improve their memory, project their voice well and use jokes or clever sayings to get an audience on their side.

The alphabet

Widespread **literacy** resulted from Greek being written with an alphabet. Our word 'alphabet' comes from the first two letters of the Greek one – *alpha* and *beta*. The Romans then used the Greek alphabet to write **Latin**. Our alphabet is based on the Latin one. An alphabet has few symbols to learn. The Greek one varied over time from 24 to 26. Each symbol stands for a single sound that can be combined with others to make more sounds. Writing systems based on representing all the sounds in a language – for example, the one used in ancient Egypt – can have tens or even hundreds of symbols to learn.

Figure it out

Greek thinkers were **pioneers** in mathematics. They also learned from the **Babylonians** and Egyptians. The basic rules and terms of **geometry** were written down by Euclid (lived around 300 BC). His textbook was still being used a hundred years ago! Other Greek mathematicians used geometry to make advances in **astronomy** and work out such problems as the **circumference** of the Earth. Despite these successes, the Greeks still used a very clumsy number system based on letters of the Greek alphabet written side by side. A four-figure number might be written using nine symbols.

This Greek coin, found at Samos, shows the famous Greek philosopher and mathematician – Pythagoras. His ideas about maths are still being used today – more than 2000 years after his death.

The calendar

Although all Greek calendars were based on the movements of the Moon, not the Sun like modern ones, every city-state had its own system, with different names for the months and varying dates for the new year. Athenian months were named after festivals held during them. Ordinary years had between 353 and 355 days and leap years had an extra month, making 383 to 385 days. Athenians also used two other calendars for deciding festival dates and dating government documents.

Arithmetic

Most Greek boys probably did not need to learn geometry, unless they wanted to become **architects**. The sons of merchants and even farmers would have to know arithmetic to trade in the market. In many Greek households wives kept the family accounts, so learning basic number skills may often have begun in the home.

Calculations were often done using a counting-board or **abacus**. This was marked in vertical columns, with the biggest units on the right and numbers marked in with pegs, counters or pebbles. Merchants' sons would probably go with their fathers on their travels. They would have to learn about different types of coinage, different systems of weights and measures – and foreign languages as well.

Telling the time

Greeks relied on sundials marked in twelve sections to show the length of daylight at a particular place. This meant that 'hours' varied in length according to the season because the length of daylight varied between summer and winter. At night or on cloudy days a water clock could be used. This let water out at a constant rate so that its level could be measured against a marked scale which represented the passing hours. Neither of these methods was very accurate but most people had no need to know the time very precisely, anyway.

Toys and games

Most ancient-Greek children's toys were easily broken or destroyed over time by damp or fire, so few have survived. Some have been found intact in the tombs of young children. Others are illustrated in paintings on vases.

Family members made most toys. Children in rich families might have toys made by skilled craftsmen. Babies were given clappers or rattles made of wood, clay pottery or bone. Some had metal bells or loose pebbles inside. Dolls were made out of cloth and wax and often had movable arms and legs. Dolls' houses and their furniture were made of wood. Model farmyard or pet animals were made out of clay, wood or bronze.

Metal hoops and wooden wheels, sometimes with bells on, were used for bowling along. Older children had spinning tops, swings and many board games. There were also wooden hobby horses, small carts with wheels similar to modern go-karts and **chariots** with sails on to go faster. Nuts were used as marbles. 'Knucklebones' was an especially popular game with girls. A set of small bones had to be tossed up with one hand and caught on the back of it.

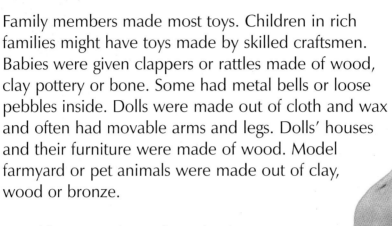

This clay doll was once a Greek child's toy. It still has moveable legs, but its arms have been lost since it was made in the 5th century BC.

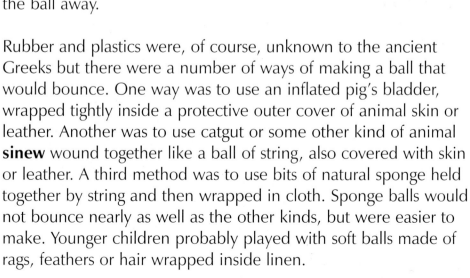

Ball games

Ancient-Greek children – and grown-ups – played many different kinds of ball game. One, played by both boys and girls, involved players being carried on one another's backs and throwing the ball to, or past, each other. Vase paintings and carvings show games that look like football and hockey, but the precise rules are unknown. Another looks like a cross between rugby and volleyball. In another, one player would throw a ball at a target – which another player tried to defend by catching or hitting the ball away.

Rubber and plastics were, of course, unknown to the ancient Greeks but there were a number of ways of making a ball that would bounce. One way was to use an inflated pig's bladder, wrapped tightly inside a protective outer cover of animal skin or leather. Another was to use catgut or some other kind of animal **sinew** wound together like a ball of string, also covered with skin or leather. A third method was to use bits of natural sponge held together by string and then wrapped in cloth. Sponge balls would not bounce nearly as well as the other kinds, but were easier to make. Younger children probably played with soft balls made of rags, feathers or hair wrapped inside linen.

Sports

The ancient Greeks took sport very seriously as part of a boy's education and military training. Sport helped boys become the sort of men Greeks admired – tough and competitive but also healthy and graceful. Sport also prepared boys for training as soldiers – encouraging strength, stamina and bravery. Every town had a gymnasium with a running track and wrestling court.

Training and being good at sport was seen as a way of honouring the gods, forming part of major festivals. There were four games – the Olympic, Isthmian, Nemean and Pythian – that drew competitors from the whole Greek world. Winners were clearly favoured by the gods who had helped them to victory. They were rewarded with statues, poems and prizes of cash or olive oil.

Each games meeting had separate competitions for boys aged twelve to seventeen in running, wrestling and boxing. Many fathers coached their sons. Former professional sportsmen became coaches when they retired. It seems that it wasn't unusual for sporting success to run in the family.

Racing
The Greeks raced both horses and horse-drawn **chariots**. Boys as well as men rode as jockeys, without **stirrups**, which were unknown to the Greeks. Boys were chosen because they were lighter than grown men.

This carving shows Greek youths playing a game that looks like hockey.

This is part of the remains of the site where the ancient- Olympic Games were held.

Chariot racing was the highest rated of all sports and one of the most dangerous. Competitors followed an oblong course, about 600 metres long, rounding a post at either end. With no barrier between chariots going in opposite directions, smashes were frequent. On one occasion only the winner finished out of 41 starters! Because chariots and horses were very expensive, racing was only for the wealthy. Ordinary people could only be spectators. The prize for winning went to the chariot's owner, not the driver who had risked his life.

Athletics

Athletic contests included sprints, long distance runs, long jump and throwing the discus or javelin. There were separate contests for girls but only sprint races. Girls wore a **tunic**, unless they were Spartans, who ran naked. Spartan girls were encouraged to play rough sports to toughen themselves for childbirth.

Combat sports

As no equipment was needed, anyone could wrestle, although there were separate competitions for boys. As there were no weight classes heavier, stronger people had an advantage. Punching was banned but breaking fingers was allowed. Wrestlers fought naked but were coated in olive oil. Boxing was less popular (except in Sparta) and even more brutal. Boxers' fists were bound with leather thongs. There were no rounds and fights went on until one fighter gave up or was knocked out.

Sickness and health

Healthy living

The ancient Greeks knew that a varied diet, fresh air, sleep and exercise were good for health. Yet even healthy people usually died by the age of 50. Children especially, died from **infectious** diseases common in summer. The biggest killer was **malaria** and, in crowded towns, **tuberculosis**. Younger children died from **dysentery** caused by poor hygiene and dirty water.

The Greeks were usually vague about population figures, except when describing the fighting force of a *polis*. Women, slaves, foreigners and children would generally be ignored so it is difficult to find accurate information about health. Although Greeks seldom bothered to put an age or cause of death on a tomb, surviving skeletons themselves provide basic evidence. **Excavations** of cemeteries suggest a high death rate in the first year after birth – probably around one child in three.

These statues show two girls playing 'knucklebones'. Girls of this age would have been lucky to survive early childhood, but they would have died young by today's standards.

If a child managed to survive to the age of three it would probably reach adulthood, although snake or insect bites, or serious burns, cuts or falls could also lead to an early death.

Helpers and healers

Most children relied on their family to treat them with traditional medicines based on herbs and natural products such as olive oil, vinegar, honey or garlic. Milk, not part of a regular diet, was often used as a medicine. Medical help was given by sellers of drugs, herbs or charms, and by midwives and gymnastic trainers as well as doctors.

Balance for health

The ancient Greeks believed four substances or 'humours' controlled the body and that when these were unbalanced, illness resulted. Bleeding, sweating and vomiting were thought to restore the balance. Medical **theory** had some **scientific** ideas but was also mixed up with belief in prayers, spells and dreams. The ancient Greeks knew nothing useful about highly-infectious diseases, such as **plague**. Young children were most vulnerable to these diseases because they were not strong enough to survive them.

Doctors

No law required doctors to be qualified, so anyone could call himself a doctor. Doctors ranked with skilled craftsmen, such as **architects**. Even the most famous Greek doctor ever, Hippocrates, admitted that over half his patients died. He warned his students that patients 'won't take medicine they don't like ... and sometimes die as a result ... and the doctor gets the blame.' Doctors knew how to set or **amputate** bones and clean and bind up cuts. Surgery was a last resort because patients usually died from the shock of the pain, loss of blood or infection afterwards.

Beliefs and behaviour

Gods

The ancient Greeks believed in many gods and thought they lived on Mount Olympus in northern Greece. Gods had to be pleased with food and gifts, animal **sacrifices** and festivals. They were like humans who fell in love, got married, had children and quarrelled. Gods also had superhuman powers, like invisibility or being able to turn into animals or foretelling the future. Each god had special interests. Artemis, goddess of hunting, wild animals and wild places, was also goddess of the Moon and childbirth. Her twin brother Apollo was god of the Sun, shepherds, music and medicine.

Rituals

Girls played an important part in many religious **ceremonies**. The ancient Greeks believed that contact with death polluted a person. It made them unfit to take part in religious ceremonies until they had been purified by washing, making a **sacrifice** and simply the passing of time.

Here a young boy is involved in a ritual act where water is poured over him.

A girl child with both parents still living – therefore unpolluted by death – was believed to be most suitable for helping priests perform **rituals**. This might involve washing the statue of a god, carrying olive branches in processions to a **temple** or grinding corn to make special cakes as offerings for the gods. Girls taking part in these rituals often came from a few aristocratic families. Boys went with their fathers to major religious occasions to learn what to do when they grew up, but they had to wait until they were old enough for military training before they had their own important part to play.

Goodness

The ancient Greeks were very interested in what it meant to be good and spent much time arguing and thinking about the question. Their ideas of goodness had little to do with religion. Gods themselves were believed to behave spitefully or wickedly. A person did not behave well to please the gods but for the sake of his reputation and the honour of his family, *phratry* and *polis*.

Learning these values would have been an important part of a child's upbringing. A good man was brave, loyal and clever. Kindness, except for generosity to friends and strangers, was not that important. Being a show-off at sport, music or speechmaking was fine, providing you had real talent to show off. Making a fool of yourself was shameful for you and your family.

Spartan values

Some of the ideas that ancient-Greek children would have learned seem strange to us now. Spartans thought that lying, cheating and stealing were useful skills, especially in time of war. Only cowardice was unforgivable. Greeks in most city-states believed that a good woman was obedient, hard-working, silent, devoted to her husband and bore many children.

Holidays and festivals

Ancient-Greek festivals were held to honour the gods. They were holidays in the sense that regular work stopped, except for essential tasks such as fetching water and feeding animals. Village children, wearing their best clothes, would come from the countryside with their families to take part in the celebrations.

Anthesteria

Each spring a festival called *Anthesteria* was held to honour Dionysus, god of wine, and to mark the passage of boys aged three, from babyhood into the first stage towards manhood. With flowers in their hair they went to a **temple** to take their first sips of wine from a small clay jug which was kept as a souvenir.

Small wine jugs like this were given to children at the *Anthesteria* festival, when they reached their third birthday.

Timetable of time off

The festival calendar followed the farmer's year, which began in July. Major celebrations marked the ploughing and sowing of the fields and later the gathering of the crops. These were supposed to make sure there would be a good harvest and plenty to eat through the year. Every *polis* also held a big festival to honour its **guardian** god or goddess, who they believed would protect the *polis* and its people. Apart from major occasions organized by the *polis* there were also many local celebrations organized by each village and ***phratry***. Adding in these minor events means that almost half the days in the year were marked by some sort of celebration or other, though not everybody would stop working for all of them. Probably about 60 festival days a year could be thought of as 'holidays' in something like the modern sense.

Festivals usually followed the same general order – a procession to a temple, the **sacrifice** of expensive animals, such as bulls, then contests and finally a feast. Women, foreigners, slaves and children could usually join in processions, although priests and older men normally went first. Sacrifice was a solemn business, with prayers. Girls were often chosen to carry the instruments used for sacrifice. Part of the sacrificed animal was left for the god, but most was set aside for the feast. Then came plays, races or wrestling, reciting of poetry and competitions between choirs or musicians, with separate contests for adults and children. Although there was a banquet, drinking and dancing, festivals were also serious. The young learned about the gods who governed their lives and the heroes they should admire.

Goodbye to childhood

For some boys, putting on their swords and helmets and beginning work as a soldier meant the end of their childhood.

Boys

Teenage boys, who had been shown to members of their father's **phratry** when they were babies, were introduced again on the third day of a three-day autumn festival called *Apaturia*. At eighteen, boys in Athens and a number of other city-states began two years military service. The first year was spent training in **barracks**; the second was spent guarding the borders of the **polis**. When they were 30 they could begin to take part in government and sit on juries.

Girls

Girls became women when they reached **puberty** and their bodies changed so that they could have babies of their own. They would go to a shrine or **temple** dedicated to the goddess Artemis and leave their favourite dolls and toys at the altar to show that their childhood was over. Quite often this happened just before a girl got married.

Marriage

Girls married in their early teens. The husband was often twice their age or more. No law required the girl to agree to the marriage and there was no need for a priest to conduct the **ceremony**. The law did usually require that both husband and wife should be **citizens** of a *polis* if their children were to be recognized as citizens of that *polis*. Husbands usually got a **dowry** of cash or land but this was a matter of custom, not law.

Weddings

The wedding ceremony began with baths in water that had been carried by children from a **sacred** spring or fountain. The bride and groom then dressed in their finest clothes for a feast at the bride's father's house. During the feast the bride took off her veil to show herself to her husband and he gave her gifts. A boy with both parents still living, then carried around a basket of bread as a sign of good luck. In the evening, the whole party went in a procession with musicians and well-wishers to the husband's house. There the newly-weds were led to the **hearth** and showered with nuts and sweets. A bride was only recognized as being truly a member of her new family, however, after she had had her first baby. This shows how important children were to the Greek family and in the role of being a wife.

This vase shows the great trouble taken to prepare a bride for her wedding.

How do we know?

Lost evidence

Most of what the ancient Greeks made is lost forever. We know homes had wooden couches – but not a single one has survived, although some bronze decorative couch-fittings have. Items made of the most common materials – wood or wax, clay or cloth, bone or leather – are most likely to have been broken, burned or to have rotted away. The same is true of papyrus or parchment documents.

Athens, Athens, Athens ...

More has survived, both written and crafted, from rich, powerful Athens than from anywhere else in the ancient-Greek world. The survival of this material, however, can distort our view of the past. In the same way it would be very difficult to study the history of the English-speaking peoples if we only had evidence of what happened in major cities like London or New York.

Marble carvings like this one, from the Parthenon in Athens, have survived over the centuries and give archaeologists vital clues about the past. Materials such as wood or cloth have not survived.

These columns in the shape of young women are known as *caryatids* and are found at many temples in Greece.

Tombs, teeth and treasures

Despite these problems we do have some hard evidence. Children's tombs often contain favourite dolls, toys and feeding bottles. They also have **inscriptions** which show how sad their parents were that they died. Their skeletons sometimes show signs of accidents or illness. Nowadays modern technology enables **archaeologists** to use tooth enamel to find out from adult skeletons whether they were ill or underfed as children.

The ancient Greeks made painted vases showing scenes from everyday life. These vases are great treasures because they are rare and beautiful – but also because they record a past that would otherwise remain lost and unknown forever. You can see many vase paintings in this book as they tell us a lot about ancient-Greek children. There is still much that we do not know about growing up in ancient Greece. We can see that life for Greek children, with its toys, games and schoolwork, shared some features of the way we live now. In fact, many parts of our lives, from school to government, would be very different without the example of ancient Greece.

Timeline

All dates are BC

c.3000	Greece controlled till c.1450 by Minoan kings based on the island of Crete
c.1600–1100	Greek-speaking Mycenaeans rule separate kingdoms in mainland Greece
c.1100–800	Period of wars and migration
c.800–700	Homer's the *Iliad* and the *Odyssey* probably composed; Greece made up of small city-states, ruled by separate kings or noble families
776	First Olympic Games
c.750–550	Greeks set up colonies in lands around Mediterranean
c.600	Coins come into use
c.500	Some city-states become democracies – Athens the most powerful
c.490–479	Main period of Persian invasions of Greece
447–432	Parthenon built on the Acropolis in Athens to honour its goddess, Athene
431–404	**Peloponnesian** War between Greek city-states, ending with Sparta eclipsing Athens as the most powerful state in mainland Greece
387	Plato founds the Academy as a school of philosophy
378–371	Sparta eclipsed by a new power – Thebes
336–323	Greece ruled by Alexander the Great of Macedon after his invasion and conquest
322	Death of Aristotle
146	Greece becomes part of the Roman Empire

Sources

▶ ◀▶ ◀▶ ◀▶ ◀▶ ◀▶ ◀▶ ◀▶ ◀▶ ◀▶ ◀▶ ◀▶ ◀▶ ◀▶ ◀▶ ◀▶ ◀▶ ◀▶

Ancient Greece, A. Pearson (Dorling Kindersley, 1992)

Ancient Olympics, R. Tames (Heinemann Library, 1996)

Children and Childhood in Classical Athens, M. Golden
(Johns Hopkins University Press, 1990)

Cultural Atlas for Young People: Ancient Greece, A. Powell (Facts on File, 1989)

Discovering the World of the Ancient Greeks, Z. Archibald (Facts on File, 1991)

The Greek Way of Life, R. Garland (Duckworth, 1990)

The Oxford Classical Dictionary, S. Hornblower and A. Spawforth
(Oxford University Press, 1996)

The Oxford History of Greece and the Hellenistic World, J. Boardman, J. Griffin
and O. Murray (Oxford University Press, 1991)

Step into Ancient Greece, R. Tames (Lorenz Books, 1999)

What Do We Know about the Greeks?, A. Pearson (Simon & Schuster, 1992)

Women's Life in Greece and Rome, M. Lefkowitz and M. Fant
(Johns Hopkins University Press, 1982)

Useful websites

www.historyforkids.org/learn/greeks/ (History for Kids)

www.worldhistorycompass.com/greek.htm (World History Compass Ancient
Greek History)

www.historylink101.com/ancient_Greece.htm (Ancient Greece History)

www.ancientgreece.com (Ancient Greece)

www.indiana.edu/-kylowack/athens/ (The Ancient City of Athens)

www.stoa.org/diotima/ (Diotoma: Women and Gender in the Ancient World)

Disclaimer

All the Internet addresses (URLs) given in this book were valid at the time of going to press.
However, due to the dynamic nature of the Internet, some addresses may have changed, or
sites may have ceased to exist since publication. While the author and publishers regret any
inconvenience this may cause readers, no responsibility for any such changes can be
accepted by either the author or the publishers.

Glossary

abacus frame with beads on for counting things

ammunition stones, arrows or other objects to be fired from weapons

amputate cut off part of the body

archaeologist person who studies objects from the past to discover how people lived

archery art of using a bow and arrows

architect person who designs buildings

astronomy study of the stars and planets

Babylonia ancient civilization based in what is now Iraq

barracks buildings where soldiers live apart from other people

brazier metal container for fire

catapult machine for firing stones or arrows

cavalry soldiers who fight on horseback

ceremony ritual performed to mark an occasion such as a birthday or a wedding

chariot two-wheeled cart used for warfare

circumference the distance around something

citizen person with the right to take part in politics

civilization distinct way of life

courtyard enclosed area surrounded by high walls

dedicated made special to or given to

democracy in the ancient-Greek world, a system of government in which all free adult males could hold office and take part in making decisions

dowry marriage gift of money, land or goods

dysentery stomach infection causing the sufferer to go to the toilet repeatedly

excavation digging to uncover buried items from the past

exile sent away, or banned, from your own country

flax plant whose fibres are made into linen

fodder food for animals

frieze carved panel running round a building

geometry branch of mathematics concerned with shapes, surfaces and solids

grazing land land with grass or plants for animals to eat

guardian person who looks after or protects

hearth place for a fire

historian person who uses written documents to discover what happened in the past

illiterate unable to read or write

infantry soldiers who fight on foot

infectious can be caught from another person

inherit be given something by a person who has died

inscription writing carved into a surface

Latin language of ancient Rome

literacy ability to read and write

lyre stringed musical instrument

malaria infectious disease spread by mosquitoes

martyr someone who dies for their religious beliefs

mess group of soldiers who share meals

military drill exercises to train soldiers to act as a team and follow orders

myth ancient story about a god or hero

oikos Greek word for household

Peloponnese southern mainland of Greece

philosopher person interested in thoughts and theories, from the Greek words meaning 'lover of knowledge'

phratrai groups of clans which were sub-divisions of the *phylae*. Each individual *phratry* was supposed to come from a shared ancestor.

phylae tribes into which Greeks were divided

physician doctor

pioneer person who goes somewhere or does something first

plague disease spread by fleas that results in death

polis Greek city-state

protein food element vital to health

puberty stage of life when the body becomes capable of having children

ritual ordered actions or gestures to worship something

ritually polluted made unfit for contact with sacred things until purified by a ceremony or the passing of time

sacred holy or concerned with the gods

sacrifice living thing killed and dedicated to the gods

scientific knowledge based in ideas proved by testing and experiments

sinew strand of muscle that attaches it to bone

statistics figures collected systematically to measure something

stirrup metal ring hung from a saddle that a rider puts his or her foot in

temple building for religious purposes

theory idea to explain something

tuberculosis infectious disease of the lungs

tunic sleeveless garment for the body, often gathered at the waist

weave intertwine fibres horizontally and vertically to make cloth

wreath circle of entwined branches

Index